A Cross-National Comparison of Effective Leadership and Teamwork

Toward a Global Workforce

A Cross-National Comparison of Effective Leadership and Teamwork

Toward a Global Workforce

Jean Brittain Leslie
Ellen Van Velsor

Center for Creative Leadership
Greensboro, North Carolina

The Center for Creative Leadership is an international, nonprofit educational institution founded in 1970 to advance the understanding, practice, and development of leadership for the benefit of society worldwide. As a part of this mission, it publishes books and reports that aim to contribute to a general process of inquiry and understanding in which ideas related to leadership are raised, exchanged, and evaluated. The ideas presented in its publications are those of the author or authors.

The Center thanks you for supporting its work through the purchase of this volume. If you have comments, suggestions, or questions about any Center publication, please contact John R. Alexander, President, at the address given below.

Center for Creative Leadership
Post Office Box 26300
Greensboro, North Carolina 27438-6300

©1998 Center for Creative Leadership

All rights reserved. No part of this publication may be reproduced, stored in a retrieval system, or transmitted, in any form or by any means, electronic, mechanical, photocopying, recording, or otherwise, without the prior written permission of the publisher. Printed in the United States of America.

CCL No. 177

Library of Congress Cataloging-in-Publication Data

Leslie, Jean Brittain.
    A cross-national comparison of effective leadership and teamwork : toward a global workforce / Jean Brittain Leslie, Ellen Van Velsor.
      p. cm.
    Includes bibliographical references.
    ISBN 1-882197-34-8
    1. Leadership—Cross-cultural studies. I. Van Velsor, Ellen. II. Title.
HD57.7.L46 1998
658.4'092—dc21   98-40879
                                                                                                                CIP

Table of Contents

Executive Summary vii

Acknowledgments ix

Introduction 1

Previous Research on Leadership Across National and Cultural Boundaries 2

Methods 4
   Research Sample 4
   Procedure 5
      Description of SYMLOG 6
      Use of the rating form 7

Results and Discussion 9
   1. E.U. and U.S. Perceptions of Effective Leadership 9
      Specific Country Comparisons of Effective Leadership 9
      Summary of Countries' Perceptions of Effective Leadership 13
   2. E.U. and U.S. Comparison of Effective Leaders to Team Members 17
      Overview of Countries' Perceptions of Effective Membership 17
      Specific Country Comparisons of Effective Leaders to Team Members 20
   3. E.U. Country Comparisons of Effective Leadership in Europe 23
      Overview of Countries' Perceptions of Effective Leadership When Working Across Europe 23
      Specific Country Comparisons of Effective Leadership When Working Across Europe 26

General Discussion and Conclusions 28
   Most Effective Leaders: Similar and Different 28
   Leader-Member Differences 29
   Working Together Across the E.U. 30
      Potential conflicts on cross-national teams 30
      Unifying cross-national teams 31

References 33

Appendix A: Previous Research on Attitude and Value Differences 35

Appendix B: Demographic Data 39

Appendix C: SYMLOG Individual and Organizational Values Rating Form 43

Appendix D: Statistical Analyses 45

Appendix E: Limitations 53

Executive Summary

This report presents the findings of a study comparing managers' perceptions of effective leadership in Europe and the U.S. Specifically, perceptions of the work-related values of effective leaders and team members in Belgium, France, Germany, Italy, Spain, U.K (European Union countries), and the U.S. were measured and analyzed for similarities and differences. The study was jointly conducted by the Center for Creative Leadership and SYMLOG Consulting Group, using SYMLOG®, a group-level assessment tool developed by Robert F. Bales, a social psychologist and professor emeritus at Harvard University.

The results support previous research, which indicates that managers in some E.U. countries perceive distinct value patterns in effective leaders from the perspective of their national work settings. Most significant, however, are new findings that show a striking consensus on what will be required of leaders and members of cross-national teams in the E.U. in the future. A value profile reflecting a delicate balance of approachable, democratic, and moderately dominant leadership that blends stability with creativity and fosters meaningful member participation in the workplace is perceived to be most effective for leadership across the E.U. in the future.

The report is written for a research-oriented human resource practitioner audience or for anyone who is interested in understanding cross-national similarities and differences in managers' perceptions of the values of effective leaders.

Acknowledgments

This research project would not have been possible without the support of corporate sponsors and the collaboration of SYMLOG Consulting Group (SCG). (SYMLOG is a registered trademark of the SYMLOG Consulting Group. The SYMLOG-related displays reproduced in this paper are used with permission.)

The following companies joined the Center for Creative Leadership (CCL) and SCG to form a research consortium to support this research: BASF AG, Colgate-Palmolive Company, DHL Worldwide Express, General Electric Company, Warner-Lambert Company, and Wilhelmsen Lines.

SCG staff Robert Koenigs, Sharon Hare, and SYMLOG consultant M. Cristina Isolabella helped to formulate the research questions, donated the SYMLOG Individual and Organizational Values Rating Forms, handled the entry of the data, and provided us with feedback on various versions of this paper. In addition, Cristina spent countless hours soliciting the participation of European managers.

Many other organizations throughout Europe helped us to collect data; and in her role at the CCL branch in Brussels, Joan Tavares also helped us find research participants in Europe.

The data-collection phase of this research was painstaking and lengthy. Edna Parrott, our project support coordinator at CCL, coded and mailed 3,665 research packets. She then helped to process the more than 1,200 forms that were returned. We thank all those managers who completed and returned SYMLOG forms.

We would also like to acknowledge the helpful comments we received on several drafts of this paper from John Alexander, Gregory Andriate, Michael Beyerlein, Michael Brannick, Jerry Brightman, Maxine Dalton, Marcia Horowitz, Sonya Prestridge, Eric Sundstrom, Walter Tornow, and Martin Wilcox.

Introduction

The globalization of business is creating new demands on individuals, organizations, and nations to work together in more and different ways. Consider, for example, the challenges that the new economic communities like the North American Free Trade Agreement (NAFTA) and the European Union (E.U.) confront in accommodating historically disparate views of how to do business.[1] The members of these communities have agreed to cooperate in a number of areas including the establishment of a single market for trade, the joint formation of foreign policy, mutual recognition of educational diplomas, and the exchange of criminal records. Through these joint efforts, they have created a new form of social organization that challenges old notions of teamwork, integration, and cooperation among people from different cultures.

As ways of doing business change significantly, the demand for managers who can perform effectively in cross-national environments increases. But what is effectiveness in the global sense? Researchers have probed extensively for the answer to this question. One particularly important area that has been investigated by Hofstede (1980a) and Trompenaars (1993) is the impact that differences in values held by individuals across cultures has on their abilities to work together effectively. For instance, how would individuals from a culture that values individualism work out business problems with individuals from a society that values collectivism?

What we don't know much about is how perspectives on *effective leadership* differ across national boundaries and how national differences affect the practice of leadership. The purpose of this paper, therefore, is to report on a research project, conducted jointly by the Center for Creative Leadership (CCL) and the SYMLOG Consulting Group, that aimed to identify similarities and differences in perceptions of effective leadership and teamwork between U.S. managers and managers from six E.U. countries (Belgium, France, Germany, Italy, Spain, and the U.K.).

SYMLOG, or the System for Multiple Level Observation of Groups, a group-level assessment tool developed by Robert F. Bales, a social psychologist and professor emeritus at Harvard University, was used to explore three sets of research questions:

---

[1] The European Union came into existence in 1993. Member states to date include: Austria, Belgium, Denmark, Finland, France, Germany, Greece, Italy, Luxembourg, Netherlands, Portugal, Republic of Ireland, Spain, Sweden, and the United Kingdom.

1. **E.U. and U.S. Perceptions of Effective Leadership:** Do the values that managers associate with effective leadership differ among E.U. countries? How do the values that U.S. managers associate with effective leadership compare with those in the E.U. countries?

2. **E.U. and U.S. Comparison of Effective Leaders to Team Members:** Are there differences between the values managers associate with leadership and the values they associate with effective membership on a team? Is there a greater difference between what is desired of leaders and members in some countries than in others?

3. **E.U. Country Comparisons of Effective Leadership in Europe:** Do the values managers associate with effective leadership within each of the E.U. countries differ from what those same managers feel would be most effective in working outside their own country on a team comprised of members from across the E.U.? To what extent will individual leaders have to change in order to be more effective in an E.U. context?

Before discussing methods and results of this study, we will first take a look at some previous research that helped guide our thinking.

A good deal of research is currently available on attitude and value differences across cultures. Some of this research (the most relevant of which is summarized in Appendix A) focuses on cross-cultural differences in managers' attitudes and values. Although these studies are important to understanding cultural differences, they do not focus on differences in how people view effective leadership.

More recent work, however, explores how value differences relate to varying perceptions of effective or desired leadership. In the next section, we will present a brief summary of some of this research on leadership across national and cultural boundaries.

Previous Research on Leadership
Across National and Cultural Boundaries

Until recently, very little research could be found that focused on how people from different nations or cultures view leadership or on how national or cultural values differences relate to differing views of effective leadership. Published studies in this area are still relatively difficult to find.

In one study, conducted by Yeung and Ready (1995), 1,200 managers from ten major global corporations in eight countries were surveyed to identify areas of similarity and difference in their views on core leadership capabilities required for effectiveness, the role of national culture in perceptions of the relative importance of these capabilities, and the best ways to develop each of the key competencies. Respondents in their study agreed that the ability to articulate a tangible vision, values, and strategy is the most important leadership capability of those listed in their questionnaire. Other key capabilities considered important by managers in most countries were "being a catalyst for strategic change," "being results-oriented," "empowering others to do their best," "being a catalyst for cultural change," and "exhibiting a strong customer orientation." They also found significant differences among countries in their assessments of the importance of most factors, with no two countries selecting identical priorities for their top five leadership capabilities. "Being a catalyst for change," for example, was seen as significantly more important in Australia than in Japan or Korea and more important in France than in Germany, Japan, or Korea. These authors conclude that there are both universal and unique aspects to leadership competency and that organizations should develop the leadership capabilities of their managers with respect to both of these needs.

Wallace (Wallace, Sawheny, & Gardjito, 1995) is one of a very few researchers who has compared valued leader characteristics across national boundaries.[2] Using mixed-gender panels of different nationalities and reviews of indigenous academic and historical literature pertaining to leader characteristics, Wallace identified 47 characteristics that incline people to willingly follow leaders. Questionnaire surveys conducted in Japan, India, Indonesia, and the United States with 409 business employees indicated that there are important national differences in characteristics that incline people to willingly follow a leader. For example, Japanese employees are significantly more inclined than employees from any of the other countries to follow a leader who is seen as profound; Indians are significantly more inclined to follow a leader who is seen as ambitious or as pragmatic; Indonesian employees are significantly more inclined to follow a leader who is seen as religious

---

[2] Another promising project, now underway, is The Global Leadership and Organizational Effectiveness Research Program (GLOBE), led by Robert J. House of The Wharton School.

or as having an authoritative bearing; and American employees report more inclination to follow leaders seen as openly and directly expressing opinions.

With respect to the relationship of desired leadership characteristics to work-related values and other social phenomena, Wallace found that 42 leader characteristics (89%) are related to national indices of work-related values, 18 (38%) are related to national economic indicators, 13 (28%) are related to religious beliefs, 7 (15%) are related to industry, 5 (11%) are related to gender, and 11 (23%) are related to family structure, ethnicity, or education. Wallace's work suggests that specific leadership characteristics that most incline people in some countries to willingly follow do not necessarily generalize to people in other countries. It also suggests that specific combinations of work-related values and economic variables may explain most of the variance in desired traits of leaders.

Methods

Research Sample

This report is based on data from middle- to upper-level English-speaking managers from Belgium, France, Germany, Italy, Spain, the U.K., and the U.S. (See Appendix B for demographic data.) Companies accepted as research sites were Fortune 500 (or equivalently large) multinational and national companies, representing diverse industries in both Europe and the U.S.

The largest percentage of the European sample ($N=1,108$) are Belgian (17%) and British (17%). The remainder are German (16%), Italian (16%), French (12%), and Spanish (9%). The majority of the sample is male (90%), with a modal age range from 40 to 49 (44%). Seventy-five percent achieved at least a university level of education. Most of the European managers sampled are upper-middle-level managers (45%) and have been practicing management for more than ten years (46%). All but 12% of the European managers have some experience working with other managers from E.U. countries.

The U.S. sample ($N=793$) was collected from CCL programs. The typical CCL program participant is male (70%), aged between 40 and 49 (40%), with at least a college degree (40%). During the time that these data were collected, participants were middle- (34%) to upper-level (33%) managers, who worked primarily in large (10,000 or more employees, 34%) industry (51%) or service (25%) organizations. Because we do not have comparable biographical data on U.S. and European managers, no additional analyses of these data were conducted. We can, however, say with confidence that the U.S. and European samples are similar in percentages of managers who are male, in the age range of 40 to 49, in educational level, and in managerial level.

Procedure

Research proposals were sent to CCL and SCG client companies who indicated an interest and willingness to participate. Following consent, research packets were mailed to a designated company contact person, or in some cases directly to the participant. Each contained a cover letter, a letter of confidentiality, a respondent demographic form, a SYMLOG Individual and Organizational Values Rating Form, and an addressed return envelope. From Greensboro, North Carolina, 3,665 research packets were mailed to European destinations. Additional telephone and written correspondence was often necessary to ensure return of these data.

SYMLOG was used to compare similarities and differences in the perceived value orientations of effective leaders and team members within seven nations. Although SYMLOG does not measure the cultural value dimensions covered in the work of Hofstede, Trompenaars, or Hampden-Turner and Trompenaars (see Appendix A for research summaries), it does what those frameworks do not do, namely to provide a model of the values associated with effective leadership.

In our study, managers were asked to fill out a form describing their demographic characteristics and to complete the English-language version of SYMLOG. (See Appendix C for a copy of the survey.) On the SYMLOG Individual and Organizational Values Rating Form, European managers were asked to rate 26 items that would yield information on the three sets of research questions:

- In general, what kinds of values does the **Most Effective LEADER** of a task-oriented group that you have actually known show in his or her behavior? (Image code in tables = MEL)

- In general, what kinds of values does the **Most Effective MEMBER** of a task-oriented group that you have actually known show in his or her behavior? (Image code in tables = MEM)

- In general, what kinds of values would be *ideal* for a person to show in his or her behavior in order to be **Most Effective** as a **LEADER** of a task-oriented team composed of individuals from various European Union countries? (Image code in tables = EML)

U.S. managers in CCL programs used only the "Most Effective Leader" and "Most Effective Member" images.

Description of SYMLOG. SYMLOG, under development at Harvard University for the last 45 years, is a comprehensive synthesis of findings, theories, and methods from psychology, social psychology, sociology, economics, political science, and several related disciplines. The theory underlying this instrument is both a "field theory" and a "systems theory." It is a systems theory in that empirical measurements are designed to take into realistic account the assumption that every pattern of behavior of an individual or a group is organically interlinked with other patterns and with a larger context. The interlinked processes have the properties of a "dynamic field" of interacting and competing tensions (Van Velsor & Leslie, 1991).

SYMLOG has been used in a wide variety of contexts and situations throughout the world. The instrument has proven reliable and valid for use by managers in the U.S. (see Leslie & Fleenor, 1998) and in many countries in Europe. Ongoing research in a variety of cultures is helping to further demonstrate its generalizability and reliability.

SYMLOG is based on a model of group dynamics that measures conflicting tensions that may enhance or inhibit effective leadership and teamwork. According to the theory, people unify around similar values and polarize around dissimilar ones. Three bipolar dimensions characterize values that can be inferred through behaviors (the instrument's 26 items). Each descriptor pair represents opposite ends of a single dimension: (1) Dominance vs. Submissiveness; (2) Friendliness vs. Unfriendliness; and (3) Acceptance of vs. Opposition to the Task-orientation of Established Authority.

The Values on Dominance vs. Values on Submissiveness dimension represents the value or importance perceived to be attached to prominence, power, status, and personal influence of an individual in relation to other group members (Bales, 1970). Dominant members tend to be active participants and tend to impose their views on the group. The more submissive members tend to be quiet and passive.

The Values on Friendly Behavior vs. Values on Unfriendly Behavior dimension is described by Bales (1970) as the value placed on an individual's

Methods 7

attitude toward the group and its goals. Friendly behavior is perceived as egalitarian, cooperative, and protective of others. Unfriendly behavior is associated with individuals who are perceived to be individualistic, self-interested, and self-protective.

The Values on Accepting the Task-orientation of Established Authority vs. Opposing Task-orientation of Established Authority dimension refers to values associated with promoting/following, or creating/changing, rules and procedures (for example, customs, norms, work demands, written rules, laws, and regulations) set up by authorities external to the work group and who will be responsible for evaluating the work group's performance.

Use of the rating form. The 26 items on the rating form (see Appendix C) are designed to measure six specific *directions* out from the center of the cube. The three-dimensional SYMLOG space can be visualized graphically with the aid of a cube model (see Figure 1, next page). Figure 1 shows the SYMLOG model as a large cube divided into smaller cubes. The cube model is a spatial representation of the three dimensions seen all at once. Out from the center, there are three double-pointed arrows that represent the six bipolar main directions: U (Upward—values on dominance), D (Downward—values on submissiveness), P (Positive—values on friendliness), N (Negative—values on unfriendliness), F (Forward—values on acceptance of authority), and B (Backward—values on nonacceptance of authority).

In addition to measuring the six main directions, the 26 items measure the portions of space between the endpoints of the arrows (see the smaller cubes in Figure 1). These smaller cubes, representing the intersections of the six directions, can be labeled using the codes for the six bipolar dimensions (U, D, P, N, F, and B). Thus, the intermediate direction between the main directions U, P, and F is labeled UPF in the upper right-hand block of the cube. The intermediate direction between F and N is labeled NF (left-middle block of the cube), and so on, all around the cube.

Each cube represents the location of a specific value type, with a corresponding type description. For example, the SYMLOG normative profile for the most effective leader and member is located in the UPF part of the space. Its corresponding value type description (based on the instrument author's empirical and theoretical work) is "often inferred from behavior perceived as purposeful democratic task leadership; correlated characteristics may include identification of self with an idealized authority, acceptance of the tasks given by authority, feeling of liking others; may be reluctant to recognize any dislike; may depend upon the power of over-idealized positive feelings to submerge, deny, or transform negative feeling and dislikes within

Figure 1
Overview of SYMLOG Three-dimensional Space®

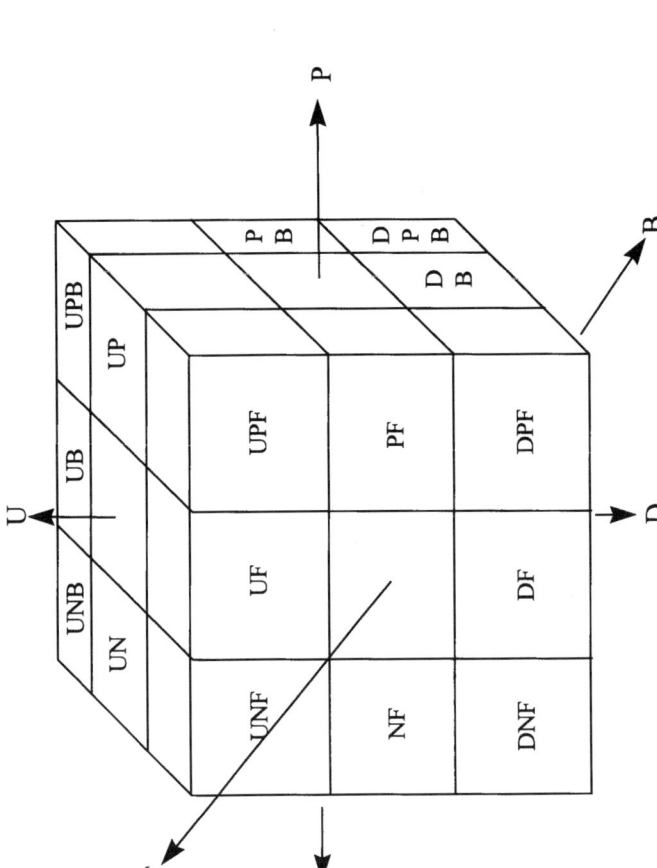

U = Values on Dominance
D = Values on Submissiveness
P = Values on Friendliness
N = Values on Unfriendliness
F = Values on Acceptance of Authority
B = Values on Nonacceptance of Authority

The cube diagram represents value positions that may be in opposition with each other. From the center of the cube there are six directions one can move: U (Upward), D (Downward), P (Positive), N (Negative), F (Forward), B (Backward). Value locations can be named by specifying their direction from the center of the space. For example, U = upward from the center; UP = upward and in a positive (right) direction. These names are used as the titles of value types.

the group; may struggle to be super-competent in spite of feelings of wanting to quit, or to show rebellious independence" (Bales, 1983).

Although these value types are derived quantitatively (by averaging a group's ratings on each of the three dimensions: U-D, P-N, F-B), the types represent a more qualitative or integrative look at the data in that they show how the three dimensions interact, resulting in different countries being in qualitatively different locations in the SYMLOG space.

Rather than go into detail here about the statistical methods used to analyze the SYMLOG data, we have placed this discussion in Appendix D.

Results and Discussion

This section is organized by research question. Within the discussion section for each question, we will present the results of several analyses of variance, allowing us to look at the degree of difference between countries on each of the three dimensions independently, and we will also present the SYMLOG type differences among countries to provide an integrative look at these data.

1. E.U. and U.S. Perceptions of Effective Leadership
Do the values that managers associate with effective leadership differ among E.U. countries? How do the values that U.S. managers associate with effective leadership compare with those in the E.U. countries?

In general, we have found that the legitimacy of grouping E.U. countries together when thinking about leadership depends on the value dimension considered. The same can be said for grouping together European countries and the U.S. Therefore, in order to answer the above two questions most effectively, we will first record the results of each country on each of the three value dimensions and comment on these results; second, we will report on the results from the value type information.

Specific Country Comparisons of Effective Leadership

Figures 2, 3, and 4 present, in simplified format,[3] the results of analyses of variance (ANOVA-Tukey's Studentized Range Test), which compared

---

[3] See Appendix D for a more detailed description of the statistical analyses.

differences in means for European and U.S. managers on the "most effective leader" (MEL) image for the three SYMLOG dimensions (dominant-submissive, friendly-unfriendly, accepting-nonaccepting [opposing] authority).

Values on Dominance vs. Values on Submissiveness. This dimension represents the prominence, power, status, and personal influence of an individual in relation to other group members. Dominant members tend to be high participators—active, engaged, and involved in the group. The more submissive members tend to be quiet and passive.

Figure 2 illustrates the three country clusters that resulted from a pairwise comparison of mean differences among the seven countries on the dominance-submissiveness dimension. As can be seen in Figure 2, all of the countries' means are positive, reflecting an overall dominant orientation to leadership.

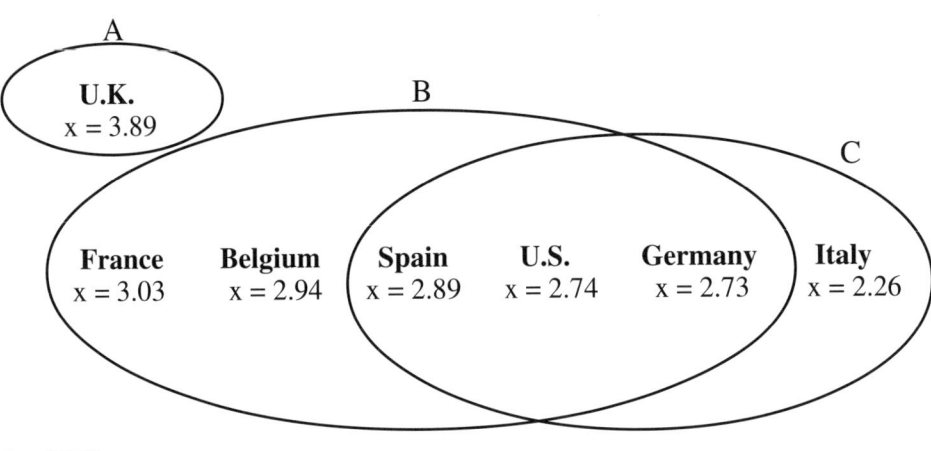

Figure 2
**Country Groupings:
Dominant Leadership Orientation**

x = mean

In Figure 2, countries located within the same circle show means that are not significantly different from each other. The overlap in circles indicates that some countries had mean values on dominance that were not different from a larger number of countries, some of whom were different from each other. For example, in Figure 2, the U.S. mean of 2.74 on dominance lies within both the circle labeled B and within the circle labeled C. That indicates that the U.S. mean is not significantly different from the means of Spain, Germany, or Italy (others co-located with the U.S. in the C circle) and it is also not significantly different from the means for France or Belgium (others co-located with the U.S. in the B circle). But the mean on dominance for France (which is in the B circle but not the C circle) is significantly different from the mean for Italy (which is included in the C circle but not the B).

Overall, the E.U. countries studied here are more alike than different on the dominance-submissiveness dimension. There are, however, a couple of variations on this theme. As can be seen in this figure, the U.K. mean for dominance is significantly different from the means of all the other countries and so the U.K. is in a circle by itself. Managers from the U.K. (3.89) view values related to dominance as more characteristic of effective leaders than do managers in most other European Union countries or in the U.S. This finding is noteworthy, since several other studies (see Ronen & Shenkar, 1985) have found a high degree of commonality between the U.S. and the U.K. on a variety of dimensions.

A second national difference in our research pertains to Italy, with Italian managers (2.26) appearing to view values related to dominance as less characteristic of effective leaders than do managers in most other European Union countries. Other countries that are close to Italy in their relatively lower valuing of an active, involved orientation among leaders are Spain, the U.S., and Germany, represented in the figure by the C circle.

Values on Friendly Behavior vs. Values on Unfriendly Behavior. The friendly-unfriendly dimension is descriptive of values relating to an individual's attitude to the group. Friendly behavior is perceived as egalitarian, cooperative, and protective of others. Behavior labeled as unfriendly is characterized as individualistic, self-interested, and self-protective.

As can be seen in Figure 3, managers in all the countries sampled perceive effective leaders to exhibit values in favor of friendly behavior. And again, managers in E.U. countries appear to be more alike than different. Yet managers in the U.S. have views that differ significantly from those of managers in the E.U. countries in that U.S. managers place the highest importance on egalitarian and cooperative values (5.53). Italian managers also differ from managers in most other E.U. countries in that they place a lower emphasis on egalitarian, cooperative values (2.93). Figure 3 shows graphically the similarities and differences on the friendly-unfriendly dimension. This finding supports the work of M. Cristina Isolabella (1992), who compared SYMLOG results of 200 North American managers to 255 Italian managers from comparable manufacturing industries. Isolabella's comparison of the value orientations of effective leaders found Italian managers to place significantly lower value than North Americans on friendly behavior.

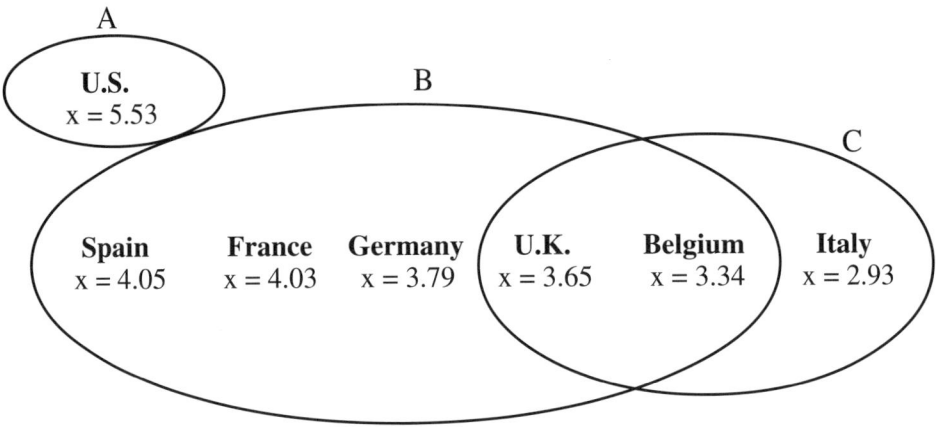

Figure 3
**Country Groupings:
Friendly Leadership Orientation**

x = mean

Values on Accepting the Task-orientation of Established Authority vs. Values on Nonacceptance (or Opposing) Task-orientation of Established Authority. This SYMLOG dimension refers to valuing the rules and procedures (for example, customs, norms, work demands, written rules, laws, regulations) set up by authorities external to the work group who will be responsible for evaluating the group's performance.

As can be seen in Figure 4, managers in all countries place a positive value on accepting the task orientation of established authority. When pairwise comparisons of the countries' means were made, three overlapping clusters of countries emerged. The group placing the highest value on accepting authority consists of the U.S., Italy, and Belgium. Isolabella (1992) also found no statistically significant difference in her study of Italian and North American managers' ratings on this dimension. The second country grouping consists of Italy, Belgium, France, and Spain. The group placing the lowest emphasis, relatively speaking, on accepting authority contains Belgium, France, Spain, Germany, and the U.K. It is noteworthy that, on this value dimension, the U.S. and the U.K. are the two countries most distant from each other.

Results and Discussion 13

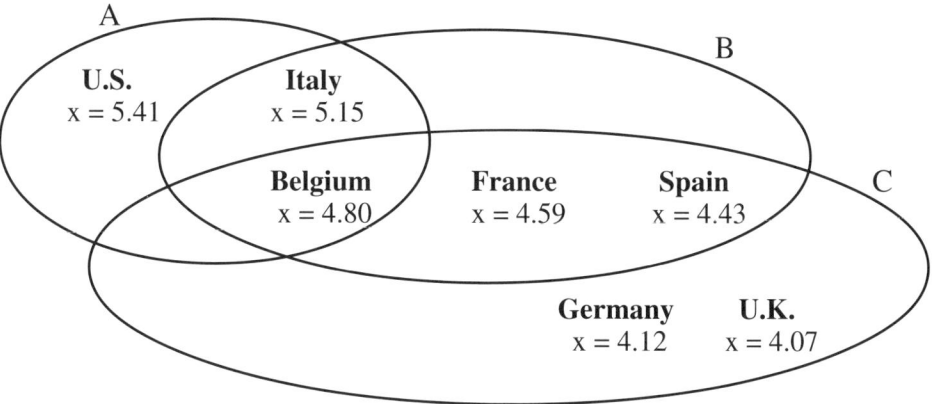

x = mean

Summary of Countries' Perceptions of Effective Leadership

As described earlier, the SYMLOG value type offers a general description of the behaviors associated with an overarching value orientation for a group (in this case, a country or national group). The final value type for each country, along with a summary descriptor, is listed in Table 1. The value type data presented here are based on the overall responses of managers to all three dimensions (dominance-submissiveness, friendly-unfriendly, accepting-nonaccepting or rejecting authority) regarding the values demonstrated in the behavior of the most effective leader they had ever known.

Although the similarity across countries lies in their placing a high value on task-oriented acceptance of authority in leaders, the variation in value type derives from the degree of joint valuing of the other two dimensions. When the three SYMLOG dimensions are considered simultaneously, it becomes clear that Belgian, German, and Italian managers are alike in that they perceive effective leaders to value, above all, the task-orientation of established authority (type F). These perceptions are probably derived from behavior that is seen as analytical, task-oriented, and problem-solving. Correlated characteristics of a task-orientation value system may include an unquestioning acceptance of the task as given and the authorized way of doing it; a serious and searching attitude toward truth or the best precedents; a constrained, persistent, and impersonal manner; continuous attention to the task with a relative lack of tolerance for diversion; and a desire to have things highly organized, well defined, and under control.

Table 1

SYMLOG Value Types for Perceptions of Effective Leadership

Country	Type	General Description
France (FR)	UPF	Active teamwork toward common goals, organizational unity: often inferred from behavior perceived as purposeful democratic task leadership.
U.K.	UF	Efficiency, strong impartial management: often inferred from behavior perceived as assertive, businesslike, and strictly impersonal.
Spain (SP)	PF	Responsible idealism, collaborative work: often inferred from behavior seen as working cooperatively with others without any obtrusive status concerns, optimism with regard to task success, and altruism with regard to others.
U.S.	PF	
Belgium (BG)	F	Conservative, established, "correct" ways of doing things: often inferred from behavior seen as strictly analytical, task-oriented, and problem-solving.
Germany (GR)	F	
Italy (IT)	F	

U=Values on Dominance, D=Values on Submissiveness, P=Values on Friendliness, N=Values on Unfriendliness, F=Values on Acceptance of Authority, B=Values on Nonacceptance of Authority

Managers from the U.K. also perceive effective leaders to value the task-orientation of established authority but favor, in addition, a dominant orientation toward leadership (type UF). A strong, dominant leadership orientation may often be assumed from behavior perceived as assertive, businesslike, and impersonal. Affiliated characteristics may include emphasis on loyalty independent of personal feelings among members; identification with an impersonal plan; a right and correct way of doing things in order to realize the plan, goal, or task prescribed for the group by higher authority; a tendency to look beyond individual differences; and a preference to adhere literally to a charted course.

Spanish and North American managers in our database are similar in that they value a task-oriented acceptance of authority in leaders along with a value system of equality and democratic participation (Type PF). Their perceptions have most likely been inferred from behavior viewed as working cooperatively with others without any obtrusive status concerns, optimism with regard to task success, and altruism with regard to others. Additional characteristics of the effective leader may include a tendency to deny or overlook domineering or unfriendly behavior in others, to feel admiration for others and see the good in them, and a tendency to agree with and to attract interaction from others in order to achieve consensus.

French managers, like other E.U. members, value task leadership, but they also prefer a balance of the other two dimensions, which in turn enhance active teamwork toward common goals (type UPF). Those valuing this leadership orientation may enjoy identifying themselves with an idealized authority, tend to accept the tasks given by authority, and demonstrate in their behavior a feeling of liking others.

Figure 5 (next page) represents a pictorial view of the SYMLOG value type differences, as well as the descriptive adjectives used to characterize the different positions of the SYMLOG space. As noted earlier, effective French leaders are perceived to fit the profile of the ideal leader (UPF); they are highly integrated, inspirational, multitalented, and well balanced. Effective leaders from Spain and the U.S. are both located in the PF part of the SYMLOG space, which typifies perceptions of effective leaders who are agreeable, attentive, cooperative, idealistic, and altruistic. The most forward country in the space, or most accepting of established authority, is the U.K. Perceptions of effective U.K. leaders would suggest individuals who are businesslike, impersonal, managerial, organized, and decisive. Findings from the remainder of the European countries—Belgium, Germany, and Italy—indicate that their managers perceive effective leaders similarly. That is, they

Figure 5
Descriptive Adjectives Characterizing Europe and the U.S. in the SYMLOG Three-dimensional Space®: Perceptions of Effective Leadership

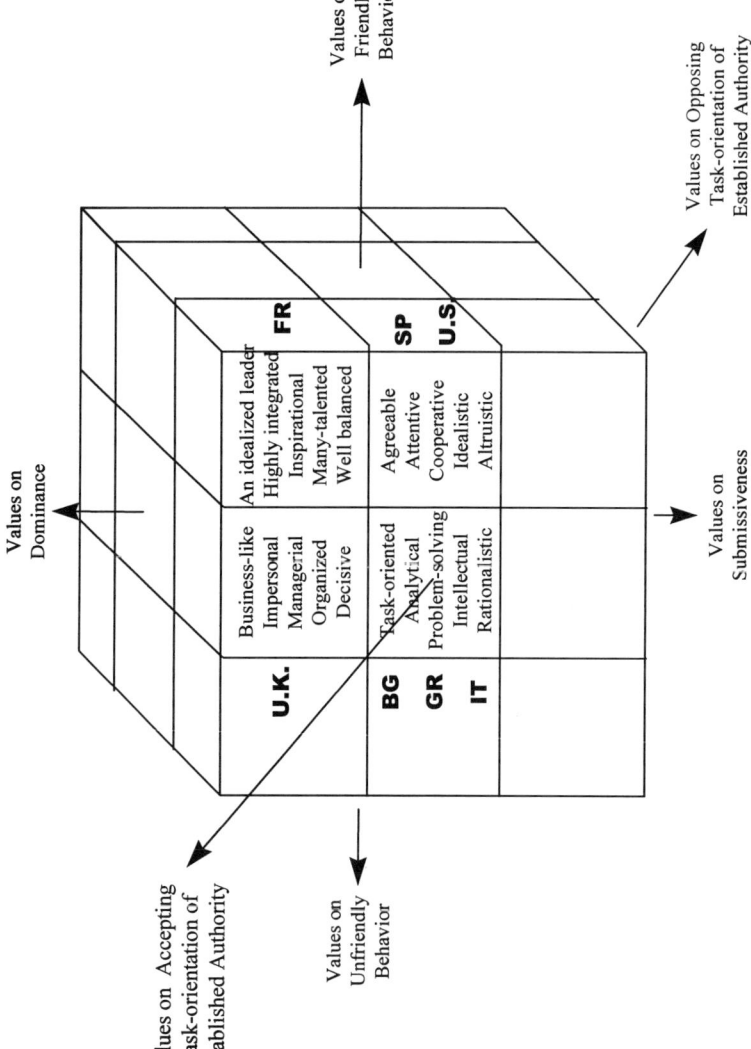

may be described as task-oriented, analytical, problem-solving, intellectual, and rationalistic.

2. E.U. and U.S. Comparison of Effective Leaders to Team Members
Are there differences between the values managers associate with leadership and the values they associate with effective membership on a team? Is there a greater difference between what is desired of leaders and members in some countries than in others?

The difference between perceptions of the values demonstrated by effective leaders and the values demonstrated by effective members can tell us something about the dynamics of work teams in different countries. This knowledge is important with respect to the increasing opportunity to work on or lead cross-national teams.

In this section we begin with a comparison of SYMLOG value types for most effective team members by country. We then address whether there is more similarity or dissimilarity between U.S. and European managers' perceptions of effective leaders and their perceptions of effective members of task-oriented groups. That is, are effective leaders seen as showing different values than effective team members and do countries vary with respect to these leader-member differences?

Overview of Countries' Perceptions of Effective Membership

SYMLOG value types for European and U.S. managers' perceptions of effective task-oriented group members are presented in Table 2. Figure 6 presents the descriptive adjectives that correspond with those final locations. U.S. managers perceive effective team members to be idealized leaders, highly integrated, inspirational, many-talented, and well balanced. As you may recall, this value type, according to the SYMLOG theory, is most reflective of those who contribute to effective leadership and teamwork. German perceptions of effective team members occupies the P, or friendly, side of the space, alone. According to the SYMLOG model, perceptions held of effective German team members might be described as friendly, egalitarian, informal, approachable, and reasonable. Our other European countries are grouped together within the PF cube. Managers' perceptions of task-oriented team members from Belgium, France, Italy, Spain, and the U.K. may be described as agreeable, attentive, cooperative, idealistic, and altruistic.

Table 2

SYMLOG Value Types for Perceptions of Effective Membership

Country	Type	General Description
U.S.	UPF	Active teamwork toward common goals, organizational unity: often inferred from behavior perceived as purposeful democratic task leadership.
Italy (IT)	PF	
Spain (SP)	PF	
U.K.	PF	Responsible idealism, collaborative work: often inferred from behavior seen as working cooperatively with others without any obtrusive status concerns, optimism with regard to task success, and altruism with regard to others.
Belgium (BG)	PF	
France (FR)	PF	
Germany (GR)	P	Equality, democratic participation in decision making: often inferred from behavior perceived as friendly, unconcerned with status differences, unafraid of disagreement.

U=Values on Dominance, D=Values on Submissiveness, P=Values on Friendliness, N=Values on Unfriendliness, F=Values on Acceptance of Authority, B=Values on Nonacceptance of Authority

Results and Discussion

Figure 6
Descriptive Adjectives Characterizing Europe and the U.S. in the SYMLOG Three-dimensional Space®: Perceptions of Effective Team Membership

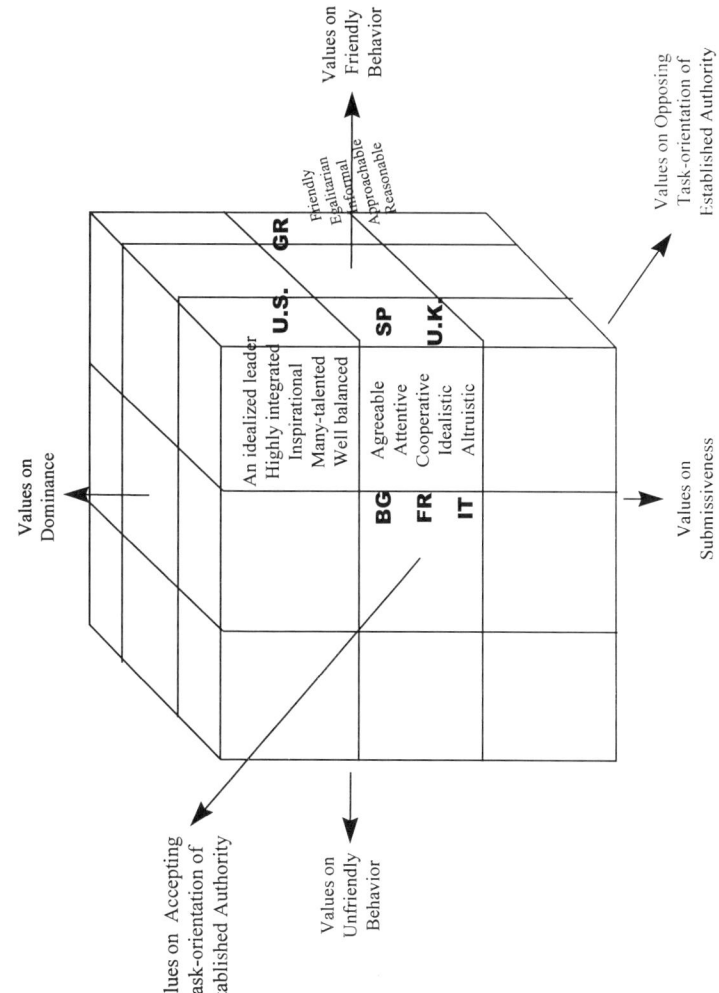

If one compares Figure 6 on the value types of effective team members to Figure 5 on the value types of effective leaders, it is clear that there are some leader-member differences within countries and that these differences may vary across countries. To explore this further, we now turn to a discussion of the analysis of variance results, comparing leader and member data by country.

Specific Country Comparisons of Effective Leaders to Team Members

Tables 3, 4, and 5 present the results of the ANOVAs using Tukey's Studentized Range Test comparing differences and similarities between the U.S. and European Union countries' value orientations toward effective leadership and team membership for each SYMLOG dimension.[4] The countries are listed from the greatest to the least difference in their perceptions of the "most effective leader" (MEL column) and the "most effective member" (MEM column) of a task-oriented group. The number in the Difference column indicates the level of statistical difference between the means on the two images.

Again, we can say overall that the results vary by SYMLOG dimension and that they support similar research (Isolabella, 1992) comparing leadership and teamwork value orientations of Italian managers and North American managers.

Values on Dominance vs. Values on Submissiveness. As can be seen in Table 3, in every one of the European countries surveyed in this study, managers perceived that effective leaders are significantly more active, engaged, and involved than effective team members. In the U.K., where effective leaders are seen as most dominant (3.89), there is also a high value on dominance among effective team members (2.20), although the difference between leaders' and members' value on dominance is a significant difference. Managers from France report the largest difference in the values on dominance of effective leaders and team members. Although French managers gave the second highest value to dominance in the behavior of an effective leader (3.03), on average, they rated effective team members as only 0.86 for dominance. And on this dimension, the results for U.S. managers are directly contrary to the European results. Among U.S. managers, effective team members are perceived to be more active, engaged, and involved (3.08) than are leaders (2.74), suggesting a very egalitarian vision for teamwork in the U.S.

---

[4] See Appendix D for a more detailed description of the statistical analyses.

Table 3
**Most Effective Leader Compared to Most Effective Member:
Values on Dominance vs. Values on Submissiveness**

Country	MEL	MEM	Difference	Probability
France	3.03	0.86	2.17	<.05
U.K.	3.89	2.20	1.69	<.05
Germany	2.73	1.21	1.52	<.05
Spain	2.89	1.53	1.36	<.05
Belgium	2.94	1.84	1.10	<.05
Italy	2.26	1.23	1.03	<.05
U.S.	2.74	3.08	(.34)	<.05

Values on Friendly Behavior vs. Values on Unfriendly Behavior.
Table 4 presents the results of the ANOVAs (using Tukey's Studentized Range Test) comparing differences and similarities between the U.S. and E.U. countries' value orientation toward leader friendliness.

Table 4
**Most Effective Leader Compared to Most Effective Member:
Values on Friendly Behavior vs. Values on Unfriendly Behavior**

Country	MEL	MEM	Difference	Probability
U.K.	3.65	5.64	(1.99)	<.05
Germany	3.79	4.81	(1.02)	<.05
Italy	2.93	3.84	(.91)	<.05
U.S.	5.53	6.21	(.68)	<.05
Belgium	3.34	3.97	(.63)	<.05
France	4.03	4.60	(.57)	ns
Spain	4.05	4.29	(.24)	ns

ns = a nonsignificant difference

In five of the seven countries (the U.K., Germany, Italy, the U.S., and Belgium), managers see effective team members as placing more emphasis on egalitarian, cooperative values (in their behaviors) than do effective leaders. Several aspects of these differences are worthy of note. First, the differences between the valuing of cooperative behaviors for leaders and team members among managers in the U.K. and Germany are greater than the differences in any other country. Second, although the difference between U.S. managers' perceptions of leader and member values on friendliness differ significantly, the U.S. managers rate a value on friendliness among team members higher than do managers in any other country (6.21). This would suggest that U.S. managers value cooperation and mutuality among team members.

Values on Accepting the Task-orientation of Established Authority vs. Values on Opposing (or Nonacceptance of) Task-orientation of Established Authority. On this SYMLOG dimension, there are statistically significant differences in only two countries (see Table 5). German and Italian managers in our sample assign more value to an acceptance of authority among effective leaders than among effective team members. In the remaining countries, there seems to be no difference between values on this dimension among effective leaders and team members. Among managers in these countries, the value placed on acceptance of authority for members tends to parallel the value placed on acceptance of authority for leaders. That is, both are relatively high in France, Belgium, Spain, the U.K., and the U.S.

Table 5
**Most Effective Leader Compared to Most Effective Member:
Values on Accepting the Task-orientation of Established Authority vs.
Values on Opposing (or Nonacceptance of) Task-orientation of
Established Authority**

Country	MEL	MEM	Difference	Probability
Germany	4.12	2.96	1.16	<.05
Italy	5.15	4.47	.68	<.05
France	4.58	4.20	.38	ns
Belgium	4.80	4.57	.23	ns
Spain	4.43	4.53	(.10)	ns
U.K.	4.07	4.39	(.32)	ns
U.S.	5.41	5.70	(.29)	ns

ns = a nonsignificant difference

3. E.U. Country Comparisons of Effective Leadership in Europe

Do the values managers associate with effective leadership within each of the E.U. countries differ from what those same managers feel would be most effective in working outside their own country on a team comprised of members from across the E.U.? To what extent will individual leaders have to change in order to be more effective in an E.U. context?

The question of whether the leadership values that managers see as important within individual E.U. countries differ from what they feel would be most effective in working across the E.U. can have important ramifications for cross-national teams.

Overview of Countries' Perceptions of Effective Leadership When Working Across Europe

When managers are asked what values typify the behavior of effective leaders of a cross-E.U. team, their responses parallel the responses related to the values shown in the behaviors of effective team members. In addition, there is a great deal of agreement across countries on both the value type and the value dimensions of leaders who are effective across national boundaries.

Table 6 presents the value type profile of the European Union countries on the SYMLOG three-dimensional model, and Figure 7 lists the descriptive adjectives that correspond with those SYMLOG types. Belgian, French, Italian, and Spanish managers indicate effective E.U. team leaders would be those individuals whose behavior reflects cooperation toward others, responsible idealism, altruism with regard to others, and optimism with regard to task success. German managers differ from Belgian, French, Italian, and Spanish managers in that German managers perceive effective leaders working across Europe to value, above all, friendly, collaborative behavior. The preference for a friendly, value-oriented leader would encourage equality and democratic participation in decision making among a culturally diverse team.

On this particular question, the U.K. moves into the "ideal" part of the SYMLOG space (type UPF). In other words, managers in the U.K. perceive effective leaders working across the E.U. to be more like the SYMLOG most effective profile for leaders and members. A U.K. leader of an E.U. team would need to show support for active teamwork toward common goals. To get a better sense of the kinds of values inferred from the behavior of effective leaders locally versus globally, see the results below.

Table 6
SYMLOG Value Types for Perceptions of Effective Leadership Working Across the E.U.

Country	Type	General Description
U.K.	UPF	Active teamwork toward common goals, organizational unity: often inferred from behavior perceived as purposeful democratic task leadership.
Belgium (BG)	PF	
France (FR)	PF	Responsible idealism, collaborative work: often inferred from behavior seen as working cooperatively with others without any obtrusive status concerns, optimism with regard to task success, and altruism with regard to others.
Italy (IT)	PF	
Spain (SP)	PF	
Germany (GR)	P	Equality, democratic participation in decision making: often inferred from behavior perceived as friendly, unconcerned with status differences, and unafraid of disagreement.

U=Values on Dominance, D=Values on Submissiveness, P=Values on Friendliness, N=Values on Unfriendliness, F=Values on Acceptance of Authority, B=Values on Nonacceptance of Authority

Figure 7
**Descriptive Adjectives Characterizing Europe and the U.S.
in the SYMLOG Three-dimensional Space®:
Perceptions of Effective Leadership When Working Across Europe**

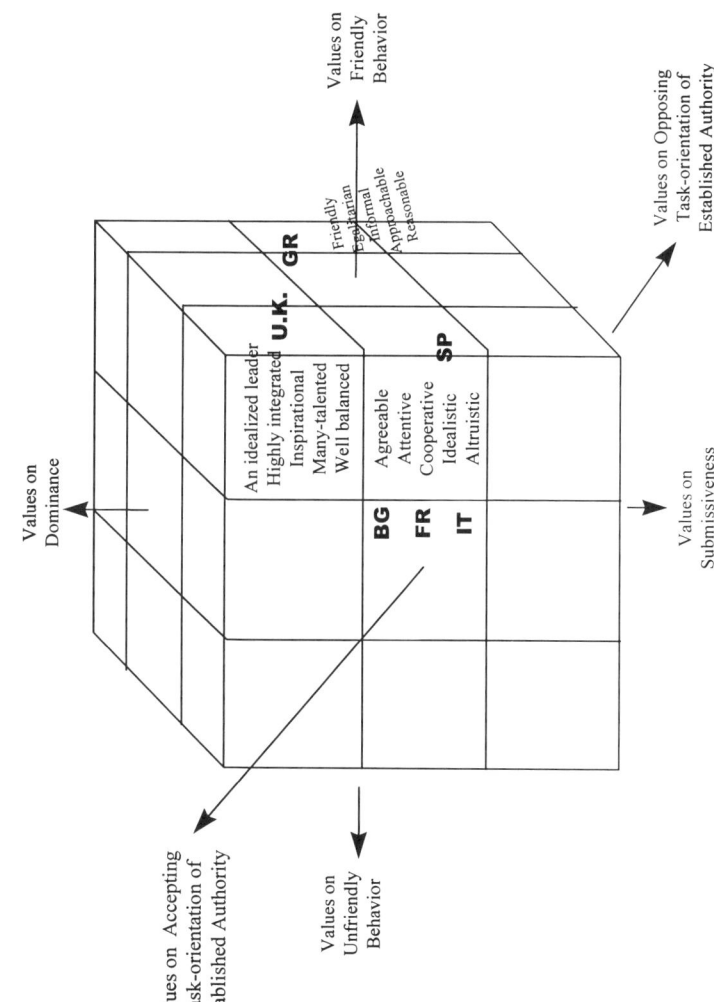

Specific Country Comparisons of Effective Leadership When Working Across Europe

The results from the statistical comparison, again, appear to differ by SYMLOG dimension. Tables 7, 8, and 9 present the results of ANOVAs (using Tukey's Studentized Range Test) that compare the values managers see underlying effective leadership in their own experience (MEL column) to the values managers see as critical to the effective leadership of a cross-national E.U. team (EML column).

Values on Dominance vs. Values on Submissiveness. Managers across Europe tend to value dominance in effective leaders they have known and in what they see as required when working with others across national (E.U.) boundaries. Spanish, Belgian, and French managers place significantly less importance on values reflecting dominance for effective leaders on an E.U. team than they do for leaders whom they perceive to have been effective locally. German and Italian managers follow a similar pattern, but not as distinctly as the other European managers sampled. Only British managers in this research perceive effective leaders as needing greater personal influence, prominence, and power over members of an E.U. team than when working within national borders.

Table 7
Most Effective European Leader Compared to E.U. Team Leader: Values on Dominance vs. Values on Submissiveness

Country	MEL	EML	Difference	Probability
Spain	2.89	2.16	.73	<.05
Belgium	2.94	2.30	.64	<.05
France	3.03	2.52	.51	<.05
U.K.	3.89	3.45	(.44)	<.05
Germany	2.73	2.38	.35	ns
Italy	2.28	2.10	.18	ns

ns = a nonsignificant difference

Values on Friendly Behavior vs. Values on Unfriendly Behavior. The results on valuing friendly behavior are clear and unidirectional. Across the board, all managers surveyed seem to agree that a high value on friendliness is important in working on a cross-national team. Of the six countries surveyed, all indicate that effective leaders of an E.U. team would need to be more open, cooperative, and egalitarian than are the effective leaders within their own countries (see Table 8).

Table 8
**Most Effective European Leader Compared to E.U. Team Leader:
Values on Friendly Behavior vs. Values on Unfriendly Behavior**

Country	MEL	EML	Difference	Probability
Italy	2.93	5.42	(2.49)	<.05
Germany	3.79	5.61	(1.91)	<.05
U.K.	3.65	5.52	(1.87)	<.05
France	4.03	5.65	(1.62)	<.05
Belgium	3.34	4.56	(1.22)	<.05
Spain	4.05	5.15	(1.10)	<.05

ns = a nonsignificant difference

Values on Accepting the Task-orientation of Established Authority vs. Values on Opposing (or Nonacceptance of) Task-orientation of Established Authority. The results for the value on acceptance of established authority are more of a mix (Table 9) than the results for the dominance-submissiveness dimension were. For half of the countries, there are no significant differences between ratings of the characteristics of most effective leaders locally and most effective leaders of an E.U. team. Only British and Spanish managers believe it necessary for effective leaders of a European team to show more value for the acceptance of authority than is needed by effective leaders within their own countries. Conversely, German managers believe leaders of a European team should place less value on task orientation than at home.

Table 9
**Most Effective European Leader Compared to E.U. Team Leader:
Values on Accepting the Task-orientation of Established Authority vs.
Values on Opposing (or Nonacceptance of) Task-orientation of
Established Authority**

Country	MEL	EML	Difference	Probability
U.K.	4.07	5.29	(1.22)	<.05
Spain	4.43	5.12	(.69)	<.05
Belgium	4.80	5.16	(.36)	ns
Italy	5.15	5.14	.01	ns
France	4.59	4.50	.09	ns
Germany	4.12	3.40	.72	<.05

ns = a nonsignificant difference

General Discussion and Conclusions

This research indicates that although differences do occur across the three dimensions measured by SYMLOG, these differences are more a matter of degree than of kind. That is, managers in all countries surveyed see at least moderate amounts of dominance, friendliness, and acceptance of authority as important aspects of effective leadership and teamwork. Yet important and subtle differences occur in the relative valuing of all three SYMLOG dimensions of teamwork when it comes to perceptions of *known effective leaders*, *known effective team members*, and the leadership required of an *effective leader of an E.U. team.*

The following remarks relate the findings from our three sets of research questions to findings in the field.

Most Effective Leaders: Similar and Different

1. E.U. and U.S. Perceptions of Effective Leadership
Do the values that managers associate with effective leadership differ among E.U. countries? How do the values that U.S. managers associate with effective leadership compare with those in the E.U. countries?

Middle- to upper-level managers in six E.U. countries (Belgium, France, Germany, Italy, Spain, and the U.K.) and in the U.S. are both similar and different in their perceptions of the value orientations of effective leaders. European and U.S. managers are similar in that they perceive effective leaders to value personal influence over the group, cooperation among the work group, and acceptance of the rules and procedures set up by authorities external to the work group. They differ in that efficiency and strong, impartial management is more highly valued among British managers, while teamwork and collaboration on the part of leaders is more highly valued among French, Spanish, and U.S. managers.

This finding points us in a similar direction as the one Yeung and Ready (1995) concluded from their study on national views of effective leadership. There are both universal and unique aspects to leadership. We found agreement among key values that managers across the E.U. and the U.S. perceive effective leaders as showing in their behavior. The magnitude of these values, however, differed across countries.

Leader-Member Differences

2. E.U. and U.S. Comparison of Effective Leaders to Team Members

Are there differences between the values managers associate with leadership and the values they associate with effective membership on a team? Is there a greater difference between what is desired of leaders and members in some countries than in others?

Comparisons of European and U.S. managers' ratings of the values of effective leaders and effective team members show few differences by country. Effective leaders of task-oriented groups are perceived to place more value on active involvement (dominance) than do effective team members in almost all of the E.U. countries sampled. However, in the U.S., managers value active involvement even more in team member behavior than they do in leader behavior. This U.S.-European difference suggests a belief in less hierarchical models of working relationships among U.S. managers and supports Hofstede's higher ranking of many of the E.U. countries on the power distance dimension. According to Hofstede (1980), hierarchical management styles tend to be more likely in countries characterized by larger degrees of power distance. And, as our research shows, more judicious use of personal prominence and power, greater openness to the ideas and interests of others, and mitigation of tough-mindedness may be more acceptable in team leaders than in members in Europe, but not in the U.S.

Values for friendliness (for example, responsible idealism and collaborative work) and acceptance of authority are seen as important in the behavior of both effective leaders and effective team members across E.U. countries.

Comparing the difference between perceptions of the values of effective team leaders and team members is an important contribution to the literature. Wallace (Wallace et al., 1995) is one of few researchers who has examined national differences in leader characteristics people willingly follow. Although Wallace's and his colleagues' research addressed "follower" expectations of leaders, our research examined perceptions of both effective leaders and followers. Our research suggests that to be effective, team members and leaders need to show similar friendly, task-oriented, work-related values in their behavior. However, expectations of team-leader dominance may vary by country.

Working Together Across the E.U.

3. E.U. Country Comparisons of Effective Leadership in Europe
Do the values managers associate with effective leadership within each of the E.U. countries differ from what those same managers feel would be most effective in working outside their own country on a team comprised of members from across the E.U.? To what extent will individual leaders have to change in order to be more effective in an E.U. context?

Potential conflicts on cross-national teams. Small but meaningful differences in value orientations can create conflict, reduce productivity, and block effective leadership on cross-national teams. Our findings suggest that subtle but definite differences do exist in the perceived values of effective leaders, among the E.U. countries and between the U.S. and E.U. countries, and that there may be some subtle shifts in behavior or value orientations required of some individuals desiring to be maximally effective on cross-E.U. teams.

One area of potential conflict might be in the different perspectives people take on the extent to which an effective leader is actively involved in group work and decision making. Groups that favor leadership that is active and dominant might perceive a leader who places a lower value on active involvement as distant or unconcerned with the group. Conversely, a group that generally places less value on the active involvement of the leader is likely to see a leader who values dominance as pushy, interfering, or not trusting of the group's ability to get the work done. In this research, managers from the U.K. are more likely than most other managers to value active individual involvement of the leader in group work and decision making. On the other hand, managers from Italy put the least emphasis on dominant, active participation in the behavior of an effective leader.

Similarly, there could be significant conflict on a team comprised of members from the U.S., where active involvement (dominance) of team members is even more highly valued than active involvement for leaders, and others from countries where the active involvement (dominance) of team members is not expected or desired. Conflict with the team leader might also be heightened if the leader does not place the same value on active involvement by members.

Differing values related to friendliness and equality can cause conflict, as well. For example, a team comprised of some members who value egalitarian leadership and cooperative work would most likely suffer a loss in productivity and innovation when led by a person who saw a more hierarchical style of leadership as appropriate.

Unifying cross-national teams. The SYMLOG model offers insight into values that can unify managers within and across nations. Organizations interested in developing leaders effective in both Europe and the U.S. might want to emphasize the importance of several shared values, while realizing that the ways in which those values play out may be country specific.

Overall, this research found a synergy in work-related values (friendliness and task orientation) that can be used as a framework to unify a team. An emphasis on cooperation, group cohesiveness, and task orientation on the part of the leader or manager is a valued commodity among members of all these nations and can lead to high team performance in a cross-European or Europe-U.S. cross-national team.

Although most European managers do not appear to strongly believe that effective leadership across countries within the European Union will require different value emphases on two of the SYMLOG dimensions (dominance-submissiveness and acceptance-nonacceptance of authority), most managers agree that, regardless of their country of origin, a high value for friendliness (more egalitarian, cooperative, protective of others) is necessary to be effective on a cross-European team. A stronger emphasis on group-oriented values would be indicated through behaviors seen as: collaborative, less individualistic, trusting in the goodness of others, protecting less able members, providing help, and involving participative decision making.

The countries that comprise the E.U. are culturally heterogeneous. They differ historically, religiously, politically, and linguistically, and, as this research supports, they differ moderately in their perceptions of leaders' and team members' work-related values. Effective cross-national teamwork among this group of powerful nations does not require extensive value changes; it can be achieved by capitalizing on the synergy already present in their understanding of how to work together. If these culturally diverse sovereign nations can use their common understanding to work effectively across borders, there is little doubt that the E.U. will provide a model of cooperation and a beacon of hope for the rest of the world.

References

Bales, R. F. (1970). *Personality and interpersonal behavior.* New York: Holt, Rinehart, and Winston.

Bales, R. F. (1983). *The SYMLOG key to individual and organizational values.* San Diego, CA: SYMLOG Consulting Group.

Cummings, L. L., Harnette, D. L., & Stevens, O. J. (1971). Risk, fate conciliation and trust: An international study of attitudinal differences among executives. *Academy of Management Journal, 14,* 285-304.

Hampden-Turner, C., & Trompenaars, A. (1993). *The seven cultures of capitalism: Value systems for creating wealth in the United States, Japan, Germany, France, Britain, Sweden, and the Netherlands* (1st ed.). New York: Currency.

Hofstede, G. (1980a). *Culture's consequences: International differences in work-related values.* Beverly Hills, CA: Sage.

Hofstede, G. (1980b). Motivation, leadership and organization: Do American theories apply abroad? *Organizational Dynamics,* pp. 42-63.

Hofstede, G., & Sami Kassem, M. (1976). *European contributions to organization theory.* Assen, Netherlands: Van Gorcum.

Isolabella, M. C. (1992). *Cross-cultural comparison of managers' team membership and leadership value orientations.* Unpublished doctoral dissertation, United States International University, San Diego, CA.

Laurent, A. (1983). The cultural diversity of western conceptions of management. *International Studies of Management and Organization, 13,* 75-96.

Leslie, J. B., & Fleenor, J. W. (1998). *Feedback to managers: A review and comparison of multi-rater instruments for management development* (3rd ed.). Greensboro, NC: Center for Creative Leadership.

Ronen, S., & Shenkar, O. (1985). Clustering countries on attitudinal dimensions: A review and synthesis. *Academy of Management Review.*

Schwartz, S. H. (1992). The universal content and structure of values: Theoretical advances and empirical tests in 20 countries. In M. P. Zanna (Ed.), *Advanced experimental social psychology,* pp. 1-65. New York: Academic Press.

Schwartz, S. H. (1994). Beyond individualism/collectivism: New cultural dimensions of values. In Kim & Hakhor (Eds.), *Individualism and collectivism: Theory, method, and applications,* pp. 85-119. Thousand Oaks, CA: Sage.

Trompenaars, F. (1993). *Riding the waves of culture.* Great Britain: Economist Books.

Van Velsor, E., & Leslie, J. B. (1991). *Feedback to managers, Volume II: A review and comparison of sixteen multi-rater feedback instruments.* Greensboro, NC: Center for Creative Leadership.

Wallace, A., Sawheny, N., & Gardjito, W. (1995). Leader characteristics that incline people to willingly follow in Japan, India, Indonesia, and the United States. In G. Tower (Ed.), *Asian Pacific international business: Regional integration and global competitiveness.* Perth, Australia: Murdoch University.

Yeung, A. K., & Ready, D. A. (1995). Developing leadership capabilities of global corporations: A comparative study in eight nations. *Human Resource Management, 34*(4), 529-547.

Appendix A:
Previous Research on Attitude and Value Differences

As people of different cultures have come into closer and more frequent contact as a result of economic, technological, and political changes over the past quarter century, researchers interested in work-related cross-cultural differences have turned their attention to differences in managers' attitudes and values. Most of their work has focused on and found differences across national boundaries. Although cultural and national boundaries are not identical by any means, knowledge about cultural value differences has enhanced the interest of researchers and practitioners in cross-national differences in effective leadership.

Cummings, Harnette, and Stevens (1971) were among the first to examine differences in attitudes of managers, focusing their attention on comparing managers from Central Europe, Spain, and the United States. Their research found that, in comparison to other managers, Americans tended to be more belligerent, risk-taking, and trusting. Americans were also found to have a higher internal locus of control.

Gerte Hofstede's research (1980a, 1980b; Hofstede & Sami Kassem, 1976) on the primary ways on which national cultures differ led to four criteria he labeled dimensions of culture: power distance, uncertainty avoidance, individualism-collectivism, and masculinity-femininity. *Power distance* is defined as the extent to which a society accepts the unequal distribution of power. *Uncertainty avoidance* describes the extent to which a society feels threatened by uncertainty and ambiguity. Those cultures characterized by a strong uncertainty avoidance would tend to create stability by establishing formal rules, not tolerating deviant ideas and behaviors, and believing in absolute truths. *Individualism-collectivism* primarily refers to in-group, out-group relations. Those societies with individualistic relations are characterized by loose-knit relations where immediate families are of utmost concern. Collectivism is characterized by a tight social network of in-group relations (relatives, clan, organizations) who look after each other and who in turn feel that they owe absolute loyalty to the group. Finally, a *masculine* society refers to one in which the values are assertive, and the acquisition for material things high. *Feminine* societies, on the other hand, are characterized by caring for the quality of life and others.

Hofstede's conclusions were based on an examination of data from 372 managers from 15 nations attending management-development programs in Switzerland and from a second sample of 60,000 respondents from a large multinational business organization in 40 countries.

André Laurent (1983) administered a 56-item management questionnaire, in English, to upper-middle-level managers attending INSEAD (the European Institute of Business Administration) programs between 1977 and 1979. This sample was comprised of 817 respondents from ten Western countries. The questionnaire was designed to test the hypothesis that the national origin of European managers significantly affects their view of what proper management should be. A factor analysis of the data produced four dimensions in which collective managerial ideologies differed: organizations as political systems, organizations as authority systems, organizations as role-formalization systems, and organizations as hierarchical-relationship systems.

Schwartz's work has played a dominant role in sorting out individual-level versus cultural-level differences in work-related values (Schwartz, 1992, 1994). His work has resulted in a circumplex model of ten universal value domains at the individual level and seven at the cultural level. Schwartz's cultural-level value types include: (1) conservatism, (2) hierarchy, (3) mastery, (4) affective and intellectual autonomy, (5) egalitarian commitment, (6) harmony, and (7) autonomy.

Trompenaars (1993) argues that people everywhere are faced with three kinds of dilemmas having to do with (1) relationships with people, (2) relationship to time, and (3) relationships between people and the natural environment. Culture, for Trompenaars, is the manner in which groups resolve these dilemmas. In his view, seven dimensions of culture are universalism-particularism, individualism-collectivism, affective-neutral, specific-diffuse, achievement-ascription, sequential-synchronic, and internal-external (the first five dimensions relate to the dilemma of relationships with people, while the sixth relates to time and the last relates to relations with the natural environment).

Trompenaars makes the point that favorite American solutions (typically based, for example, on preferences for universalism, individualism, neutrality, specificity, and achievement in relation to people) will not be seen as solutions to these dilemmas in other cultures. Because at least five of Trompenaars' dimensions relate to relationships among people and because leadership is primarily about relationships, it may be that cultural values have an impact on the leadership orientations that people perceive as effective.

In addition, Hampden-Turner and Trompenaars (1993) identified seven fundamental valuing processes upon which they believe wealth-creating organizations are based: (1) universalism-particularism, (2) analyzing-integrating, (3) individualism-group, (4) inner direction-outer direction, (5) time as a sequence-time as synchronization, (6) achieved status-ascribed status, and (7) equality-hierarchy. Their research on 15,000 managers having international responsibilities from around the world indicates that national differences are significant even among this population.

Appendix B:
Demographic Data

Table B1
Number of European Respondents Used in Data Analysis

Country	N	% of Total
Belgium	221	17
U.K.	215	17
Germany	209	16
Italy	202	16
France	148	12
Spain	113	9
Missing	5	0

Table B2
Sex of European Respondents

Sex	N	% of Total
Male	1143	90
Female	130	10
Missing	2	0

Table B3
Age of European Respondents

Age	N	% of Total
20-29	59	5
30-39	367	29
40-49	559	44
50-59	262	20
60+	24	2
Missing	4	0

Table B4
Educational Level of European Respondents

Education	N	% of Total
High School	186	15
Gymnasium	111	9
University	679	53
Post-university	284	22
Missing	15	1

Table B5
Organizational Level of European Respondents

Organizational Level	N	% of Total
Top (senior or CEO, managing director)	74	6
Director (VP, executive or board professional)	262	21
Upper-middle (dept. executive, plant manager, senior professional)	578	45
Middle (office manager, professional staff, middle-level administrator)	332	26
Other	24	2
Missing	5	0

Appendix B

Table B6
Years of Managerial Experience Among European Residents

Years of Managerial Experience	N	% of Total
Less than 2 years	94	7
2-5 years	256	20
6-10 years	345	27
More than 10 years	574	46
Missing	6	0

Table B7
Level of Experience Working with Other European Managers

E.U. Experience	N	% of Total
None	158	12
Some	123	10
Moderate	508	40
High	239	19
Very High	246	19
Missing	1	0

Appendix C:
SYMLOG Individual and Organizational Values Rating Form

DESCRIPTIVE ITEMS—Individual and Organizational Values

		CODE NAME 1 MEL	CODE NAME 2 MEM	CODE NAME 3 CUR	CODE NAME 4 EML
U	1 Individual financial success, personal prominence and power				
UP	2 Popularity and social success, being liked and admired				
UPF	3 Active teamwork toward common goals, organizational unity				
UF	4 Efficiency, strong impartial management				
UNF	5 Active reinforcement of authority, rules, and regulations				
UN	6 Tough-minded, self-oriented assertiveness				
UNB	7 Rugged, self-oriented individualism, resistance to authority				
UB	8 Having a good time, releasing tension, relaxing control				
UPB	9 Protecting less able members, providing help when needed				
P	10 Equality, democratic participation in decision making				
PF	11 Responsible idealism, collaborative work				
F	12 Conservative, established, "correct" ways of doing things				
NF	13 Restraining individual desires for organizational goals				
N	14 Self-protection, self-interest first, self-sufficiency				
NB	15 Rejection of established procedures, rejection of conformity				
B	16 Change to new procedures, different values, creativity				
PB	17 Friendship, mutual pleasure, recreation				
DP	18 Trust in the goodness of others				
DPF	19 Dedication, faithfulness, loyalty to the organization				
DF	20 Obedience to the chain of command, complying with authority				
DNF	21 Self-sacrifice if necessary to reach organizational goals				
DN	22 Passive rejection of popularity, going it alone				
DNB	23 Admission of failure, withdrawal of effort				
DB	24 Passive non-cooperation with authority				
DPB	25 Quiet contentment, taking it easy				
D	26 Giving up personal needs and desires, passivity				

R = RARELY   S = SOMETIMES   O = OFTEN

SYMLOG Consulting Group
18580 Polvera Dr.
San Diego, CA 92128
(619) 673-2098

Copyright © 1983 by Robert F. Bales

Research Survey

You will answer FOUR (4) questions on this form. It is NOT necessary to complete the identification section on the other side of this form.

Focus: Please consider your experience with very effective LEADERS of task-oriented work groups in a business setting. Think about a person that represents the "Most Effective" LEADER of a work group you have actually known. Reflect on how this person interacted with other members of the work group, particularly when they were together as a team. Keep this person in mind as you answer the question below.

Question 1. In general, what kinds of values does the Most Effective LEADER of a task-oriented group that you have actually known show in his or her behavior?

To answer this question, turn this page over and locate the column labeled CODE NAME 1 MEL. Mark your responses with a No. 2 pencil.

Go **down** the column marking R = Rarely, S = Sometimes, or O = Often for each of the 26 descriptive items. NOT ALL OF THE ITEMS MAY SEEM TO GO TOGETHER. IF EVEN ONE ITEM FITS, USE IT AS YOUR GUIDE.

When you have finished marking all 26 items in column 1 (MEL) please answer the following:

Focus: Please consider your experience with very effective MEMBERS of task-oriented work groups in a business setting. Think about a person that represents the "Most Effective" MEMBER of a work group you have actually known. Reflect on how this person interacted with other members of the work group, particularly when they were together as a team. Keep this person in mind as you answer the question below.

Question 2. In general, what kinds of values does the Most Effective MEMBER of a task-oriented group that you have actually known show in his or her behavior?

When you have finished marking all 26 items in column 2 (MEM) please answer the following:

Focus: Please consider your organization and the way members interact with you, each other, and with customers. Reflect on the organizational philosophy, policies, and procedures as these are played out on a daily basis over time. Keep these reflections in mind as you answer the question below.

Question 3. In general, what kinds of values are CURRENTLY shown in the culture of your organization?

When you have finished marking all 26 items in column 3 (CUR) please answer the following:

Focus: Whether or not you have actually worked on such a team, please consider a task-oriented team composed of individuals from various European Community countries. Reflect on how this work team might be culturally diverse in its make-up and how these group members are likely to interact, particularly when they are together as a team. Keep these reflections in mind as you answer the question below.

Question 4. In general, what kinds of values would be ideal for a person to show in his or her behavior in order to be Most Effective as a LEADER of a task-oriented team composed of individuals from various European Community countries?

(Mark your responses down the column labeled CODE NAME 4 EML.)

When you have completed the form, please return it to the appropriate person. Thank you.

Appendix D:
Statistical Analyses

To answer questions about *most effective leadership* (MEL) and *most effective membership* (MEM), respondents indicated for each of the 26 descriptive phases whether the phrase is associated with the question rarely, sometimes, or often. The 26 descriptive phases are probes for the 26 vectors that can be mathematically combined to measure three bipolar SYMLOG dimensions. For our analyses of responses among countries, we analyzed the three dimensions separately using a One-Way ANOVA[1] (SAS statistical software–General Linear Models for unbalanced designs) and used Tukey's[2] Studentized Range (HSD) Test to cluster responses according to each of the three SYMLOG dimensions. Figures 2-4 present the results of these tests graphically in a nontraditional academic manner. For a more traditional display, see Tables D1-D6 on the following pages.

---

[1] Hayes, W. L. (1988). *Statistics.* Chicago: Holt Rinehart & Winston, Inc.
[2] *SAS/STAT User's Guide* (Version 6, 4th ed.). Cary, NC: SAS Institute.

Table D1
Dimension Means by SYMLOG Image
MOST EFFECTIVE LEADER

Country	Dimension	N	Mean	Std Dev
Belgium	Dominance/Submissiveness	221	2.94	3.06
	Friendly/Unfriendly		3.34	4.25
	Accepting/Nonaccepting		4.80	3.39
France	Dominance/Submissiveness	148	3.03	3.11
	Friendly/Unfriendly		4.03	4.10
	Accepting/Nonaccepting		4.59	3.79
Germany	Dominance/Submissiveness	209	2.73	2.83
	Friendly/Unfriendly		3.79	3.92
	Accepting/Nonaccepting		4.12	3.34
Italy	Dominance/Submissiveness	202	2.26	2.99
	Friendly/Unfriendly		2.93	3.99
	Accepting/Nonaccepting		5.15	3.78
Spain	Dominance/Submissiveness	113	2.89	3.08
	Friendly/Unfriendly		4.05	3.83
	Accepting/Nonaccepting		4.43	3.20
U.K.	Dominance/Submissiveness	215	3.89	3.04
	Friendly/Unfriendly		3.65	4.09
	Accepting/Nonaccepting		4.07	3.56
U.S.	Dominance/Submissiveness	793	2.74	3.07
	Friendly/Unfriendly		5.53	3.47
	Accepting/Nonaccepting		5.41	3.43

Appendix D

Table D2
Dimension Means by SYMLOG Image
MOST EFFECTIVE MEMBER

Country	Dimension	N	Mean	Std Dev
Belgium	Dominance/Submissiveness	221	1.84	2.90
	Friendly/Unfriendly		3.97	4.00
	Accepting/Nonaccepting		4.57	3.77
France	Dominance/Submissiveness	148	0.86	2.98
	Friendly/Unfriendly		4.60	3.48
	Accepting/Nonaccepting		4.20	3.70
Germany	Dominance/Submissiveness	209	1.21	3.01
	Friendly/Unfriendly		4.81	4.07
	Accepting/Nonaccepting		2.96	3.42
Italy	Dominance/Submissiveness	202	1.23	3.32
	Friendly/Unfriendly		3.84	3.57
	Accepting/Nonaccepting		4.47	3.75
Spain	Dominance/Submissiveness	113	1.53	3.54
	Friendly/Unfriendly		4.29	3.50
	Accepting/Nonaccepting		4.53	3.30
U.K.	Dominance/Submissiveness	215	2.20	3.08
	Friendly/Unfriendly		5.64	3.47
	Accepting/Nonaccepting		4.39	3.37
U.S.	Dominance/Submissiveness	793	3.08	2.82
	Friendly/Unfriendly		6.21	3.45
	Accepting/Nonaccepting		5.70	3.52

Table D3
Dimension Means by SYMLOG Image
EFFECTIVE LEADERSHIP WORKING ACROSS THE E.U.

Country	Dimension	N	Mean	Std Dev
Belgium	Dominance/Submissiveness	221	2.30	2.82
	Friendly/Unfriendly		4.56	3.26
	Accepting/Nonaccepting		5.16	3.04
France	Dominance/Submissiveness	148	2.52	2.83
	Friendly/Unfriendly		5.65	2.97
	Accepting/Nonaccepting		4.50	2.85
Germany	Dominance/Submissiveness	209	2.38	3.00
	Friendly/Unfriendly		5.61	3.41
	Accepting/Nonaccepting		5.42	3.24
Italy	Dominance/Submissiveness	202	2.10	2.66
	Friendly/Unfriendly		5.42	3.24
	Accepting/Nonaccepting		5.14	3.36
Spain	Dominance/Submissiveness	113	2.16	3.31
	Friendly/Unfriendly		5.15	3.21
	Accepting/Nonaccepting		5.12	3.26
U.K.	Dominance/Submissiveness	215	3.45	2.53
	Friendly/Unfriendly		5.52	3.25
	Accepting/Nonaccepting		5.29	3.33

Table D4
ANOVA Comparing European Countries' and U.S. Managers' Value Orientations Toward Most Effective Leader for Dominance vs. Submissiveness

Country	Mean	Tukey Grouping
U.K.	3.89	A
France	3.03	B
Belgium	2.94	B
Spain	2.89	B C
U.S.	2.74	B C
Germany	2.73	B C
Italy	2.26	C

Table D5
ANOVA Comparing European Countries' and U.S. Managers' Value Orientations toward Most Effective Leader for Friendly Behavior vs. Unfriendly Behavior

Country	Mean	Tukey Grouping
U.S.	5.53	A
Spain	4.05	B
France	4.03	B
Germany	3.79	B
U.K.	3.65	B C
Belgium	3.34	B C
Italy	2.93	C

Table D6
ANOVA Comparing European Countries' and U.S. Managers' Value Orientations toward Most Effective Leader for Acceptance vs. Nonacceptance

Country	Mean	Tukey Grouping
U.S.	5.41	A
Italy	5.15	A B
Belgium	4.80	A B C
France	4.59	B C
Spain	4.43	B C
Germany	4.12	C
U.K.	4.07	C

To answer questions comparing team role *most effective leadership* (MEL) to *most effective membership* (MEM), and *effective leadership working across the E.U.* (EML), we analyzed the three dimensions separately using a repeated measures One-Way ANOVA (SAS statistical software– General Linear Models for unbalanced designs) and used Tukey's Studentized Range (HSD) Test to cluster responses according to each of the three SYMLOG dimensions. Tables D7-D12 report the results of the models for MEL & MEM and MEL & EML comparisons.

Table D7
**Most Effective Leader Compared to Most Effective Member:
Values on Dominance vs. Values on Submissiveness**

Country	MEL Mean	MEM Mean	DF	F Value	F
France	3.03	0.86	1	54.97	<.0001
U.K.	3.89	2.20	1	50.10	<.0001
Germany	2.73	1.21	1	48.61	<.0001
Spain	2.89	1.53	1	15.44	<.0001
Belgium	2.94	1.84	1	22.66	<.0001
Italy	2.26	1.23	1	14.78	<.001
U.S.	2.74	3.08	1	8.26	<.05

Table D8
**Most Effective Leader Compared to Most Effective Member:
Values on Friendly Behavior vs. Values on Unfriendly Behavior**

Country	MEL Mean	MEM Mean	DF	F Value	F
U.K.	3.65	5.64	1	35.38	<.0001
Germany	3.79	4.81	1	10.61	<.001
Italy	2.93	3.84	1	7.58	<.01
U.S.	5.53	6.21	1	15.34	<.0001
Belgium	3.34	3.97	1	4.80	<.05
France	4.03	4.60	1	2.39	ns
Spain	4.05	4.29	1	.55	ns

ns = a nonsignificant difference

Appendix D

Table D9
**Most Effective Leader Compared to Most Effective Member:
Values on Accepting the Task-orientation of Established Authority vs. Values on Opposing (or Nonacceptance of) Task-orientation of Established Authority**

Country	MEL Mean	MEM Mean	DF	F Value	F
Germany	4.12	2.96	1	19.84	<.0001
Italy	5.15	4.47	1	5.06	<.05
France	4.58	4.20	1	.92	ns
Belgium	4.80	4.57	1	.64	ns
Spain	4.43	4.53	1	.14	ns
U.K.	4.07	4.39	1	1.34	ns
U.S.	5.41	5.70	1	2.81	ns

ns = a nonsignificant difference

Table D10
**Most Effective European Leader Compared to E.U. Team Leader:
Values on Dominance vs. Values on Submissiveness**

Country	MEL Mean	EML Mean	DF	F Value	F
Spain	2.89	2.16	1	5.45	<.05
Belgium	2.94	2.30	1	10.61	<.001
France	3.03	2.52	1	4.10	<.05
U.K.	3.89	3.45	1	4.43	<.05
Germany	2.73	2.38	1	2.69	ns
Italy	2.28	2.10	1	.49	ns

ns = a nonsignificant difference

Table D11
**Most Effective European Leader Compared to E.U. Team Leader:
Values on Friendly Behavior vs. Values on Unfriendly Behavior**

Country	MEL Mean	EML Mean	DF	F Value	F
Italy	2.93	5.42	1	72.91	<.0001
Germany	3.79	5.61	1	39.30	<.0001
U.K.	3.65	5.52	1	35.44	<.0001
France	4.03	5.65	1	25.13	<.0001
Belgium	3.34	4.56	1	17.15	<.0001
Spain	4.05	5.15	1	10.15	<.01

Table D12
**Most Effective European Leader Compared to E.U. Team Leader:
Values on Accepting the Task-orientation of Established Authority vs. Values on Opposing (or Nonacceptance of) Task-orientation of Established Authority**

Country	MEL Mean	EML Mean	DF	F Value	F
U.K.	4.07	5.29	1	20.10	<.0001
Spain	4.43	5.12	1	6.26	<.05
Belgium	4.80	5.16	1	2.37	ns
Italy	5.15	5.14	1	.05	ns
France	4.59	4.50	1	.06	ns
Germany	4.12	3.40	1	8.80	<.01

ns = a nonsignificant difference

Appendix E:
Limitations

This research was based on a survey of managers' perceptions. While this type of research has value, it can offer little understanding of causality. In other words, these data offer a snapshot of what E.U. and U.S. managers perceive to be values for effective leaders and team members, but they can do little to explain why or how.

The survey form itself presents several problems. First, it was not translated into the native language of the respondents. We can assume that in some cases the fact that English was not the primary language caused difficulty. Second, some of our respondents may have been unfamiliar with the process of completing scannable questionnaires like SYMLOG. In fact, we received an inquiry from a French company as to what was meant by a number-2 pencil. These managers' responses may have been affected by their confidence in completing the form.

Finally, our samples were based on voluntary participation. Because we were unable to randomly sample the countries of interest, these data lack generalization beyond our samples. We do not know, for example, if the views of those who chose not to participate are drastically different from those who did.

The reader might also note that it is not our intent to stereotype cultures or people. The results presented here are based on people's perceptions of values underlying behavior; it is not meant to say that this is the way people from a particular culture will act.

In general, these data can be used to refer to general perceptions within the countries where we collected data. Through the SYMLOG leadership and teamwork model, this research offers a guide into the kind of development necessary for teams working within and across nations.

CENTER FOR CREATIVE LEADERSHIP PUBLICATIONS

SELECTED REPORTS:

The Adventures of Team Fantastic: A Practical Guide for Team Leaders and Members G.L. Hallam (1996, Stock #172) $20.00

CEO Selection: A Street-smart Review G.P. Hollenbeck (1994, Stock #164) $25.00

Choosing 360: A Guide to Evaluating Multi-rater Feedback Instruments for Management Development E. Van Velsor, J. Brittain Leslie, & J.W. Fleenor (1997, Stock #334) $15.00

Creativity in the R&D Laboratory T.M. Amabile & S.S. Gryskiewicz (1987, Stock #130) $12.00

A Cross-National Comparison of Effective Leadership and Teamwork: Toward a Global Workforce J.B. Leslie & E. Van Velsor (1998, Stock #177) $15.00

Eighty-eight Assignments for Development in Place: Enhancing the Developmental Challenge of Existing Jobs M.M. Lombardo & R.W. Eichinger (1989, Stock #136) $15.00

Enhancing 360-degree Feedback for Senior Executives: How to Maximize the Benefits and Minimize the Risks R.E. Kaplan & C.J. Palus (1994, Stock #160) $15.00

Evolving Leaders: A Model for Promoting Leadership Development in Programs C.J. Palus & W.H. Drath (1995, Stock #165) $15.00

Forceful Leadership and Enabling Leadership: You Can Do Both R.E. Kaplan (1996, Stock #171) $15.00

Formal Mentoring Programs in Organizations: An Annotated Bibliography C.A. Douglas (1997, Stock #332) $20.00

Four Essential Ways that Coaching Can Help Executives R. Witherspoon & R.P. White (1997, Stock #175) $10.00

Gender Differences in the Development of Managers: How Women Managers Learn From Experience E. Van Velsor & M.W. Hughes (1990, Stock #145) $35.00

A Glass Ceiling Survey: Benchmarking Barriers and Practices A.M. Morrison, C.T. Schreiber, & K.F. Price (1995, Stock #161) $15.00

Helping Leaders Take Effective Action: A Program Evaluation D.P. Young & N.M. Dixon (1996, Stock #174) $18.00

How to Design an Effective System for Developing Managers and Executives M.A. Dalton & G.P. Hollenbeck (1996, Stock #158) $15.00

Inside View: A Leader's Observations on Leadership W.F. Ulmer, Jr. (1997, Stock #176) $12.00

The Intuitive Pragmatists: Conversations with Chief Executive Officers J.S. Bruce (1986, Stock #310) $12.00

Leadership for Turbulent Times L.R. Sayles (1995, Stock #325) $15.00

A Look at Derailment Today: North America and Europe J. Brittain Leslie & E. Van Velsor (1996, Stock #169) $20.00

Making Common Sense: Leadership as Meaning-making in a Community of Practice W.H. Drath & C.J. Palus (1994, Stock #156) $15.00

Managerial Promotion: The Dynamics for Men and Women M.N. Ruderman, P.J. Ohlott, & K.E. Kram (1996, Stock #170) $15.00

Managing Across Cultures: A Learning Framework M.S. Wilson, M.H. Hoppe, & L.R. Sayles (1996, Stock #173) $15.00

Perspectives on Dialogue: Making Talk Developmental for Individuals and Organizations N.M. Dixon (1996, Stock #168) $20.00

Preventing Derailment: What To Do Before It's Too Late M.M. Lombardo & R.W. Eichinger (1989, Stock #138) $25.00

The Realities of Management Promotion M.N. Ruderman & P.J. Ohlott (1994, Stock #157) $15.00

Selection at the Top: An Annotated Bibliography V.I. Sessa & R.J. Campbell (1997, Stock #333) ... $20.00

Should 360-degree Feedback Be Used Only for Developmental Purposes? D.W. Bracken, M.A. Dalton, R.A. Jako, C.D. McCauley, V.A. Pollman, with Preface by G.P. Hollenbeck (1997, Stock #335) $15.00

Succession Planning: An Annotated Bibliography L.J. Eastman (1995, Stock #324) $20.00

Training for Action: A New Approach to Executive Development R.M. Burnside & V.A. Guthrie (1992, Stock #153) $15.00

Twenty-two Ways to Develop Leadership in Staff Managers R.W. Eichinger & M.M. Lombardo (1990, Stock #144) $15.00

Using 360-degree Feedback in Organizations: An Annotated Bibliography J.W. Fleenor & J.M. Prince (1997, Stock #338) $15.00
Using an Art Technique to Facilitate Leadership Development C. De Ciantis (1995, Stock #166) ... $15.00
Why Managers Have Trouble Empowering: A Theoretical Perspective Based on Concepts of Adult Development W.H. Drath (1993, Stock #155) $15.00

SELECTED BOOKS:
Balancing Act: How Managers Can Integrate Successful Careers and Fulfilling Personal Lives J.R. Kofodimos (1993, Stock #247) $28.00
Beyond Ambition: How Driven Managers Can Lead Better and Live Better R.E. Kaplan, W.H. Drath, & J.R. Kofodimos (1991, Stock #227) $32.95
Breaking Free: A Prescription for Personal and Organizational Change D.M. Noer (1997, Stock #271) $25.00
Breaking the Glass Ceiling: Can Women Reach the Top of America's Largest Corporations? (Updated Edition) A.M. Morrison, R.P. White, & E. Van Velsor (1992, Stock #236A) $13.00
Choosing to Lead (Second Edition) K.E. Clark & M.B. Clark (1996, Stock #327) $25.00
Discovering Creativity: Proceedings of the 1992 International Creativity and Innovation Networking Conference S.S. Gryskiewicz (Ed.) (1993, Stock #319) $30.00
Executive Selection: A Look at What We Know and What We Need to Know D.L. DeVries (1993, Stock #321) $20.00
Healing the Wounds: Overcoming the Trauma of Layoffs and Revitalizing Downsized Organizations D.M. Noer (1993, Stock #245) $29.50
High Flyers: Developing the Next Generation of Leaders M.W. McCall, Jr. (1997, Stock #293) $27.95
If I'm In Charge Here, Why Is Everybody Laughing? D.P. Campbell (1984, Stock #205) $9.95
If You Don't Know Where You're Going You'll Probably End Up Somewhere Else D.P. Campbell (1974, Stock #203) $9.95
Inklings: Collected Columns on Leadership and Creativity D.P. Campbell (1992, Stock #233) $15.00
Leadership: Enhancing the Lessons of Experience (Second Edition) R.L. Hughes, R.C. Ginnett, & G.J. Curphy (1996, Stock #266) $55.00
The Lessons of Experience: How Successful Executives Develop on the Job M.W. McCall, Jr., M.M. Lombardo, & A.M. Morrison (1988, Stock #211) $24.95
Making Diversity Happen: Controversies and Solutions A.M. Morrison, M.N. Ruderman, & M. Hughes-James (1993, Stock #320) $20.00
The New Leaders: Guidelines on Leadership Diversity in America A.M. Morrison (1992, Stock #238) $32.00
Readings in Innovation S.S. Gryskiewicz & D.A. Hills (Eds.) (1992, Stock #240) $25.00
Selected Research on Work Team Diversity M.N. Ruderman, M.W. Hughes-James, & S.E. Jackson (Eds.) (1996, Stock #326) $24.95
Staying on Track L.D. Coble & D.L. Brubaker (1997, Stock #280) $18.95
Take the Road to Creativity and Get Off Your Dead End D.P. Campbell (1977, Stock #204) $9.95
The Working Leader: The Triumph of High Performance Over Conventional Management Principles L.R. Sayles (1993, Stock #243) $20.00

SPECIAL PACKAGES:
Development and Derailment (Stock #702; includes 136, 138, & 144) $35.00
The Diversity Collection (Stock #708; includes 145, 177, 236A, 238, 317, & 320) $85.00
Executive Selection (Stock #710; includes 141, 321, 333, & 157) $50.00
Gender Research (Stock #716; includes 145, 161, 170, 236A, & 238) $90.00
HR Professional's Info Pack (Stock #717; includes 136, 158, 165, 169, 324, & 334) $75.00
New Understanding of Leadership (Stock #718; includes 156, 165, & 168) $40.00
Personal Growth, Taking Charge, and Enhancing Creativity (Stock #231; includes 203, 204, & 205) $20.00

Discounts are available. Please write for a comprehensive Publications catalog. Address your request to: Publication, Center for Creative Leadership, P.O. Box 26300, Greensboro, NC 27438-6300, 336-545-2805, or fax to 336-545-3221. All prices subject to change.

ORDER FORM

Or E-mail your order via the Center's online bookstore at www.ccl.org

Name _____ Title _____

Organization _____

Mailing Address _____
(street address required for mailing)

City/State/Zip _____

Telephone _____ FAX _____
(telephone number required for UPS mailing)

Quantity	Stock No.	Title	Unit Cost	Amount

CCL's Federal ID Number is 237-07-9591.

Subtotal _____

Shipping and Handling _____
(add 6% of subtotal with a $4.00 minimum; add 40% on all international shipping)

NC residents add 6% sales tax; CA residents add 7.75% sales tax; CO residents add 6.2% sales tax

TOTAL _____

METHOD OF PAYMENT
(ALL orders for less than $100 must be PREPAID.)

❏ Check or money order enclosed (payable to Center for Creative Leadership).

❏ Purchase Order No. _____ (Must be accompanied by this form.)

❏ Charge my order, plus shipping, to my credit card:
　　❏ American Express　❏ Discover　❏ MasterCard　❏ VISA

ACCOUNT NUMBER: _____ EXPIRATION DATE: MO. ___ YR. ___

NAME OF ISSUING BANK: _____

SIGNATURE _____

❏ Please put me on your mailing list.

Publication • Center for Creative Leadership • P.O. Box 26300
Greensboro, NC 27438-6300
336-545-2805 • FAX 336-545-3221

fold here

PLACE
STAMP
HERE

CENTER FOR CREATIVE LEADERSHIP
PUBLICATION
P.O. Box 26300
Greensboro, NC 27438-6300